CW00369742

cute
cake pops

Women's Weekly
THE AUSTRALIAN

contents

Whenever I take cake pops to a party, they disappear in minutes. Everyone just loves these fun, colourful, easy-to-eat treats. Most can be made a day or two ahead, and look fabulous on the party table. Try making simpler ones at first, take your time, and you'll soon become an expert.

Pamela Clark

Editorial & Food Director

before you begin

Cake pops are fiddly to make, but well worth the effort. Allow yourself plenty of time and call on family or friends to help you decorate and make it a fun occasion. Choose a simple cake pop to start with and once you've mastered that you'll be ready to tackle slightly trickier versions.

GETTING STARTED

• Most of these cake pops are decorated with supermarket staples, however a trip to a good cake decorating supplier will inspire you and can make decorating easier. If you don't have a store near you, try ordering decorations online.

• Once balls of cake are coated with icing or melted chocolate, they need to dry without touching any surface. Stand the pops upright in a thick styrofoam block, available from cake decorating suppliers. If you can't find styrofoam, use some old egg cartons. Make holes in the top with a skewer or small knife, just large enough to hold the sticks upright. You will need to make sure you have this in place before you start dipping the cake pops.

• Cake pop sticks (also sold as "lollipop candy sticks") are available from cake decorating suppliers and craft shops. You can also use paddle pop sticks, available from some newsagents, bamboo skewers (remove the pointed end) or even swirly plastic straws.

THE CAKE

• For each recipe, we have suggested a type of cake to suit the style of cake pop. Feel free to choose your own, but avoid anything too dry or light in texture. Varieties that work well are firm-textured butter, coconut, mud or fruit cakes. Leftover Christmas cakes and puddings work well too, as they're usually moist.

• To keep the preparation time to a minimum, we have mostly used shop-bought cakes.

• Discard any icing or filling unless specified, then crumble the cake with your hands into a large bowl. Pack it firmly into metric cup measures.

- As some cakes will differ in moisture content and texture, you may find that your cake crumbs weigh or compress differently to ours when measuring and rolling the ball shapes. This may give you a different number of cake pops. Simply adjust the size of the cake pops if needed, or you may find you have extras.
- The freezer is a great help when preparing cake pops, as it chills and firms the mixture quickly. You can refrigerate cake pops instead if you don't have the freezer space, just allow more time.

DECORATING

- For most of the coating we used compound chocolate buds or "Melts". These are much easier to work with than eating chocolate, and the cake pops will keep their shape at room temperature.

- Note that white chocolate is a creamy yellow colour; if you want a white coating, you will need to purchase Candy Melts (different to chocolate Melts) from cake decorating suppliers. Candy Melts are also available in colours.
- When tinting white chocolate, remember that because you are starting with a cream-coloured base, the resulting colour may not be true. An example is rose pink colouring – it will turn a salmon colour when added to white chocolate. If you need to match a particular colour, use Candy Melts.
- We recommend using paste food colourings. Add just a little at a time.
- Products are available from cake decorating suppliers that stabilise chocolate when tinting, and thin the chocolate, making dipping easier.

- If working with a large number of cake pops, it is best to take one batch at a time out of the freezer or fridge.
- You may need to re-melt the chocolate every now and again if it begins to thicken.

STORING

- Most cake pops can be made at least two days before the party.
- Store pops at a cool, dry room temperature.
- Most cake pops will be firm enough, once set, to place lying down, in a single layer, in an airtight container. This makes them easy to store and transport.
- If you find they are a little soft, keep them standing up in styrofoam or egg cartons and cover them with an upturned box or container to keep them dust-free.

rocky road pops

- 300g (9½ ounces) chocolate brownies
- 1 cup (170g) firmly packed butter cake crumbs
- ⅓ cup (100g) ready-made chocolate frosting
- ¼ cup (15g) mini mallows, halved
- ¼ cup (50g) red glacé cherries, chopped coarsely
- ¼ cup (35g) roasted unsalted peanuts, chopped coarsely
- 100g (3 ounces) dark (semi-sweet) eating chocolate, chopped
- 24 lollipop or paddle pop sticks
- ½ cup (40g) flaked almonds

1 Break brownies into small crumbs in a medium bowl. Using a fork, combine brownie crumbs, cake crumbs and frosting.
2 Stir in mini mallows, cherries and peanuts until combined. Roll level tablespoons of the mixture into balls. Place balls on a baking paper-lined tray, freeze 1 hour or refrigerate 3 hours or overnight, until firm.
3 Stir chocolate in a small heatproof bowl over a small saucepan of simmering water until smooth (don't let water touch base of bowl). Pour into a heatproof jug.
4 Dip the end of one stick into the chocolate, then push it about halfway into a ball of cake. Return to tray. Repeat with remaining sticks and balls of cake. Freeze for about 5 minutes to set.

5 Meanwhile, toast almonds, by stirring them over medium heat in a medium frying pan, until golden brown. Transfer to a small heatproof bowl; cool.
6 Re-melt the chocolate if necessary. Dip the top half of each cake pop into melted chocolate, then into toasted almonds. Stand pops upright in a styrofoam block (see page 4) until set.

makes 24
prep + cook time 40 minutes (+ freezing & standing)
store cake pops in an airtight container at a cool room temperature until ready to serve. They will keep for up to a week.

tips Ready-made brownies can be found in the bakery section of most supermarkets.

Eat Me!

tip Cake pops without green calyxes will keep refrigerated for up to 2 days.

strawberry cheesecake pops

- 360g (11½ ounces) frozen strawberry cheesecake, thawed
- 2½ cups (425g) firmly packed butter cake crumbs
- 375g (12 ounces) white chocolate Melts
- red food colouring
- 18 lollipop or paddle pop sticks
- 18 green drinking straws
- ⅓ cup (1½ ounces) green sprinkles
- 50g (1½ ounces) ready-made white icing
- green food colouring
- cornflour (cornstarch)

makes 18
prep + cook time 1½ hours
(+ freezing & standing)

1 Using a fork, combine cheesecake, including biscuit base, and cake crumbs in a medium bowl. Roll level tablespoons of the mixture into strawberry shapes. Place on a baking paper-lined tray, freeze 1 hour or refrigerate 3 hours or overnight, until firm.
2 Stir chocolate in a medium heatproof bowl over a medium saucepan of simmering water until smooth (don't let water touch base of bowl). Tint chocolate red. Pour into a heatproof jug.
3 Dip the end of one stick into the chocolate, then push it about halfway into a strawberry shape. Return to tray. Repeat with remaining sticks and strawberries. Freeze for about 5 minutes to set.

4 Dip one cake pop into the chocolate, rocking back and forth to coat; don't swirl the pop, or it'll break. Allow excess chocolate to drip back into the jug. Slide a straw over the stick, pushing up into the chocolate. Stand pop upright in a styrofoam block (see page 4); scatter with sprinkles. Repeat with remaining cake pops, chocolate, straws and sprinkles. Re-melt chocolate as necessary.
5 Tint icing green, knead on a surface lightly dusted with cornflour until it loses its stickiness. Roll onto lightly dusted surface until icing is 3mm (⅛ inch) thick. Using a 2.5cm (1-inch) star cutter, cut 18 stars from rolled out icing. Working quickly, use a frilling tool to frill edges of stars, making them look like calyxes. Thread frilled leaves onto sticks, securing with a little melted chocolate.

little lions

- 2½ cups (400g) firmly packed chocolate mud cake crumbs
- ½ cup (150g) ready-made milk chocolate frosting
- 375g (12 ounces) white chocolate Melts
- orange food colouring
- 22 lollipop or paddle pop sticks
- 3 orange fruit sticks (10g)
- 22 brown Smarties (25g)
- 88 yellow Smarties (90g)
- 66 orange Smarties (65g)
- 66 red Smarties (65g)
- 132 x 2.5cm (1-inch) lengths vermicelli noodles
- ¼ quantity royal icing (see page 74)
- black food colouring

makes 22
prep + cook time 1 hour
(+ freezing & standing)

1 Combine cake crumbs and frosting in a medium bowl. Using wet hands, shape level tablespoons of mixture into balls, squeezing firmly. Place on a baking paper-lined tray; freeze 1 hour or refrigerate 3 hours or overnight, until firm.

2 Melt white chocolate in a medium heatproof bowl over a medium saucepan of simmering water until smooth (don't let water touch base of bowl); tint chocolate pale orange. Pour into a heatproof jug.

3 Dip the end of one stick into chocolate, then push it about halfway into a ball of cake. Return to tray. Repeat with remaining sticks and balls of cake. Freeze for about 5 minutes to set.

4 Meanwhile, cut 22 small triangles from fruit sticks for noses. Cut brown Smarties in half; attach to the top of pops with a little of the chocolate to make ears. Stand until set.

5 Dip one cake pop into the chocolate, covering ears, rocking back and forth to coat; don't swirl the pop, or it'll break. Allow excess chocolate to drip back into the jug. Stand cake pop upright in a styrofoam block (see page 4) until set. Repeat with remaining cake pops. Re-melt chocolate as necessary.

6 Cut an edge from each of the remaining Smarties; attach them to pops with a little chocolate for the mane. To make whiskers, attach six vermicelli pieces to each pop; top with fruit stick triangles for a nose. Stand pops upright until set.

7 Tint royal icing black. Spoon icing into a small piping bag fitted with a 3mm (⅛-inch) tube. Pipe on eyes and mouth.

tips Store cake pops in an airtight container at a cool room temperature until ready to serve. They will keep for up to a week. Pipe eyes and mouths on the day of serving. Don't refrigerate, as colouring on Smarties will run. Buy about 500g (1 pound) Smarties to get the colours we've used, or choose your own colours.

tips Store cake pops in an airtight container at a cool room temperature until ready to serve. They will keep for up to a week. Don't refrigerate, or the colouring in the Smarties will run.

cute cake pops

- 350g (11-ounce) banana cake with frosting
- 375g (12 ounces) white chocolate Melts
- sky blue, rose pink and lemon yellow food colouring
- 12 lollipop or paddle pop sticks
- 400g (12½ ounces) ready-made white icing
- cornflour (cornstarch)
- 1 tablespoon coloured sprinkles
- 1 tablespoon hundreds and thousands
- 12 red Smarties

makes 12
prep + cook time
1½ hours
(+ freezing & standing)

1 Process cake and frosting until mixture just comes together. Push tablespoons of the mixture firmly into a 12-hole (1-tablespoon/20ml) mini muffin pan. Place pan in the freezer, freeze 1 hour.

2 Carefully remove cakes from pan using a flat-bladed knife. Reshape cakes, if necessary.

3 Stir chocolate in a medium heatproof bowl over a medium saucepan of simmering water until smooth (don't let water touch base of bowl). Divide chocolate evenly between three small bowls; tint pale blue, pink and yellow.

4 Dip the end of one stick into the chocolate, then push it about halfway into the base of a cake. Return to tray. Repeat with remaining sticks and cakes, alternating chocolate colours. Freeze for about 5 minutes to set.

5 Dip one cake pop into the chocolate, rocking back and forth to coat; don't swirl the pop, or it'll break. Allow excess chocolate to drip back into the jug. Stand pop upright in a styrofoam block (see page 4) until set. Repeat with remaining cake pops and chocolate, alternating colours (you will have four pops in each colour). Re-melt chocolate as necessary.

6 Divide icing into three balls. Tint icing pale blue, pink and yellow. Wrap in plastic. Dust a surface lightly with cornflour. Unwrap blue icing and roll into a 5mm (2-inch) sausage. Cut into four equal lengths. Brush the top of four cake pops with a little water. Wrap icing in a spiral on tops of pops. Repeat with remaining icings.

7 Lightly brush icing with a little water, scatter with sprinkles and hundreds and thousands. Re-melt chocolate if necessary. Use a little chocolate to secure Smarties to tops of cakes.

Valentine's Day love hearts

- 4 cups (640g) firmly packed chocolate cake crumbs
- ⅓ cup (100g) ready-made chocolate frosting
- 275g (9 ounces) white chocolate Melts
- red food colouring
- 28 lollipop or paddle pop sticks
- 1 tablespoon each pink and red heart-shaped sprinkles
- 14 sugar hearts

makes 28
prep + cook time 55 minutes (+ freezing & standing)
store cake pops in an airtight container at a cool room temperature until ready to serve. They will keep for up to a week.

1 Grease and line a deep 15cm (6-inch) square cake pan with baking paper. Combine cake crumbs and frosting in a medium bowl. Press mixture evenly into the pan; cover; freeze 1 hour or refrigerate 3 hours or overnight, until firm.

2 Using a 4.5cm (1¾-inch) heart-shaped cutter, cut 28 hearts from the cake mixture. Place on a baking paper-lined tray, freeze 1 hour, or refrigerate 3 hours or overnight, until firm.

3 Stir chocolate in a medium heatproof bowl over a medium saucepan of simmering water until smooth (don't let water touch base of bowl); tint red. Pour into a heatproof jug.

4 Dip the end of one stick into chocolate, then push the stick about halfway into a cake heart. Repeat with remaining sticks and hearts. Return to tray. Place in freezer for about 5 minutes to set.

5 Dip one cake pop into the chocolate, rocking back and forth to coat; don't swirl the pop, or it'll break. Allow excess chocolate to drip back into the jug. Scatter pop with combined sprinkles. Stand upright in a styrofoam block (see page 4) until set. Repeat with remaining cake pops, decorating another 13 with sprinkles, and attaching sugar hearts to the other 14 with a little of the melted chocolate. Stand upright until set.

tip Use red Candy Melts in place of tinted chocolate Melts, if you like.

tips Store cake pops in an airtight container at a cool room temperature until ready to serve. They will keep for up to a week. Use skewers, lollipop or paddle pop sticks in place of toothpicks if you like.

choc-caramel mud pops

- 180g (5½ ounces) white eating chocolate, chopped
- 4½ cups (540g) firmly packed caramel mud cake crumbs
- 375g (12 ounces) milk chocolate Melts
- 25 cocktail toothpicks
- ¼ cup (50g) chocolate sprinkles

1 Stir white chocolate in a medium heatproof bowl over a medium saucepan of simmering water until smooth (don't let water touch base of bowl).

2 Stir melted chocolate into cake crumbs. Using wet hands, shape rounded tablespoons of the mixture into balls, squeezing firmly. Place on a baking paper-lined tray. Freeze 1 hour or refrigerate 3 hours or overnight, until firm.

3 Stir milk chocolate in a medium heatproof bowl over a medium saucepan of simmering water until smooth (don't let water touch base of bowl). Pour into a heatproof jug.

4 Dip the end of one toothpick into the chocolate, then push it about halfway into a ball of cake. Return to tray. Repeat with remaining toothpicks and balls of cake. Place into the freezer for about 5 minutes to set.

5 Dip one cake pop into the chocolate, rocking back and forth to coat; don't swirl the pop, or it'll break. Allow excess chocolate to drip back into the jug; scatter with sprinkles. Stand pop upright in a styrofoam block (see page 4) until set. Repeat with remaining cake pops, chocolate and sprinkles. Re-melt chocolate as necessary.

makes 25
prep + cook time
40 minutes
(+ freezing & standing)

Christmas snowmen

- 1½ cups (240g) firmly packed white chocolate mud cake crumbs
- 1 tablespoon ready-made vanilla frosting
- 225g (7 ounces) white chocolate Melts
- 16 lollipop or paddle pop sticks
- ⅓ cup (25g) desiccated coconut
- 8 orange fruit sticks
- 8 black licorice tubes
- 60cm (23½-inch) long licorice strap

makes 16
prep + cook time 1 hour (+ freezing & standing)
store cake pops in an airtight container at a cool room temperature until ready to serve. They will keep for up to a week.

1 Using a fork, combine cake crumbs and frosting in medium bowl. Shape tablespoons of mixture into balls, squeezing firmly. Place balls on a baking paper-lined tray. Freeze 1 hour or refrigerate 3 hours or overnight, until firm.

2 Stir chocolate in a medium heatproof bowl over a medium saucepan of simmering water until smooth (don't let water touch base of bowl). Pour into a heatproof jug.

3 Dip the end of one stick into the chocolate, then push it about halfway into a ball of cake. Return to tray. Repeat with remaining sticks and balls of cake. Freeze for about 5 minutes to set.

4 Dip one cake pop into the chocolate, rocking back and forth to coat; don't swirl the pop, or it'll break. Allow excess chocolate to drip back into the jug. Sprinkle pop with coconut. Stand cake pop upright in a styrofoam block (see page 4) until set. Repeat with remaining cake pops, chocolate and coconut. Re-melt chocolate as necessary.

5 Cut fruit sticks in half, then cut one end of each into a point for "carrot" noses. Attach noses with a little of the chocolate.

6 Cut licorice tubes in half. Using a 1.5cm (¾-inch) cutter, cut 16 rounds from licorice strap. Secure cut licorice tubes to licorice rounds with a little chocolate to create hats. Cut remaining licorice into small pieces for eyes and mouths. Secure with chocolate. Stand upright until set.

tip Use white Candy Melts in place of chocolate Melts for an extra-white finish.

tip You can use any flavoured jelly you wish.

coconut raspberry jelly pops

- 4 cups (680g) firmly packed butter cake crumbs
- ⅓ cup (100g) ready-made vanilla frosting
- 85g (3 ounces) raspberry jelly crystals
- 50g (1½ ounces) white chocolate Melts
- 30 lollipop sticks or bamboo skewers
- 1 cup (80g) desiccated coconut
- 30 coloured drinking straws

makes 30
prep + cook time 45 minutes (+ freezing & refrigeration)
store cake pops in an airtight container in the fridge until ready to serve. They will keep for up to a week.

1 Using a fork, combine cake crumbs and frosting in a medium bowl. Roll level tablespoons of mixture into balls. Place balls on a baking paper-lined tray, freeze 1 hour or refrigerate 3 hours or overnight, until firm.

2 Make jelly according to packet instructions; pour into a shallow baking pan. Refrigerate for about an hour or until jelly has thickened slightly.

3 Stir chocolate in a small heatproof bowl over a small saucepan of simmering water until smooth (don't let water touch base of bowl). Dip the end of one stick into the chocolate, then push it halfway into a ball of cake. Return to tray. Repeat with remaining sticks and balls of cake. Freeze for about 5 minutes to set.

4 Transfer partially-set jelly to a small bowl or jug; place coconut in another small bowl. Dip one cake pop into jelly; rocking back and forth to coat; don't swirl the pop, or it'll break. Allow excess jelly to drip back into the jug. Dip pop in coconut to cover jelly completely. Stand cake pop upright in a styrofoam block (see page 4). Repeat with remaining cake pops, jelly and coconut. Refrigerate until set.

5 Carefully slide straws over sticks, pushing them up into pops until they feel secure.

brownie bombs

- 75g (2½ ounces) butter, chopped coarsely
- 100g (3 ounces) dark eating (semi-sweet) chocolate, chopped coarsely
- ⅓ cup (75g) caster (superfine) sugar
- 1 egg
- ⅔ cup (100g) plain (all-purpose) flour
- 2 tablespoons dark rum
- 375g (12 ounces) dark chocolate Melts
- 30 lollipop or paddle pop sticks
- 2 tablespoons (28g) Choc Pearls

makes 30
prep + cook time 1 hour (+ cooling, freezing & standing)

1 Preheat oven to 180°C/350°F. Grease a deep 18cm (7¼-inch) square cake pan; line base and sides with baking paper.
2 Stir butter and chopped chocolate in a small saucepan over low heat until smooth; transfer to a medium bowl, cool 10 minutes.
3 Stir sugar, egg and flour into chocolate mixture. Spread into pan; bake about 20 minutes. Cool in pan.
4 Cut cake into large pieces; using a food processor, process cake with rum until mixture just comes together. Shape rounded teaspoons of the mixture into balls. Place on a baking paper-lined tray. Freeze 1 hour or refrigerate 3 hours or overnight, until firm.

5 Stir chocolate Melts in a medium heatproof bowl over a medium saucepan of simmering water until smooth (don't let water touch base of bowl). Pour into a heatproof jug.
6 Dip the end of one stick into the chocolate, then push it about halfway into a ball of cake. Return to tray. Repeat with remaining sticks and balls of cake. Freeze for about 5 minutes to set.
7 Dip one cake pop into the chocolate, rocking back and forth to coat; don't swirl the pop, or it'll break. Allow excess chocolate to drip back into the jug. Stand on a baking paper-lined oven tray; sprinkle with Pearls before chocolate sets. Repeat with remaining cake pops and Pearls. Stand at room temperature until set. Serve in paper cases.

tip Store cake pops in an airtight container at a cool room temperature until ready to serve. They will keep for up to a week.

note Ginger kisses are small cream-filled sponge cakes, about 25g (¾ ounce) each.

gingerbread men

- 400g (12½ ounces) ginger kisses
- 375g (12 ounces) white chocolate Melts
- brown and orange food colouring
- 8 paddle pop sticks
- 1 quantity royal icing (see page 74)
- 24 red mini M&M's

makes 8
prep + cook time
1 hour 10 minutes
(+ freezing & standing)
store cake pops in an airtight container at a cool room temperature until ready to serve. They will keep for up to a week.

1 Crumble kisses (with filling) into a medium bowl. Using hands, knead the mixture into a ball. Roll the mixture between sheets of baking paper to a 1.5cm (¾-inch) thickness. Transfer, on baking paper, to tray; refrigerate 20 minutes.

2 Using a 9cm (3¾-inch) cutter, cut out as many gingerbread men as possible. Re-roll mixture to cut out a total of eight men. Place on baking paper-lined trays; freeze 1 hour or refrigerate 3 hours or overnight, until firm.

3 Stir chocolate in a medium heatproof bowl over a medium saucepan of simmering water until smooth (don't let water touch base of bowl). Tint light brown using brown and orange colouring. Pour into a heatproof jug.

4 Dip 4.5cm (1¾ inches) of the end of one paddle pop stick into chocolate; place coated end of paddle pop stick over back of gingerbread man, pressing lightly until beginning to set. Return to tray. Repeat with remaining sticks and gingerbread men. Place in freezer for about 5 minutes to set.

5 Re-melt chocolate if necessary. Working quickly, hold a gingerbread man over the jug of chocolate; spoon chocolate over man to cover. Allow excess chocolate to drip back into the jug. Stand cake pop upright in a styrofoam block (see page 4) until set. Repeat with remaining men and chocolate.

6 Spoon royal icing into a piping bag fitted with 4mm (¼-inch) tube. Pipe around outline of men. Pipe face and secure three M&M's to each gingerbread man for buttons. Stand at room temperature until set.

baby rattles

- 4 cups (680g) firmly packed butter cake crumbs
- ½ quantity buttercream (see page 75)
- 375g (12 ounces) white chocolate Melts
- 30 lollipop sticks or bamboo skewers
- 30 striped drinking straws
- ½ quantity royal icing (see page 74)
- blue, pink and yellow food colouring

makes 30
prep + cook time
1 hour 20 minutes
(+ freezing & standing)
store cake pops in an airtight container at a cool room temperature until ready to serve. They will keep for up to a week.

1 Using a fork, combine cake crumbs and about ½ cup of the buttercream in a medium bowl, until ingredients come together.

2 Shape level tablespoons of the mixture into balls, squeezing firmly. Place balls on a baking paper-lined tray; freeze 1 hour or refrigerate 3 hours or overnight, until firm.

3 Stir chocolate in a medium heatproof bowl over a medium saucepan of simmering water until smooth (don't let water touch base of bowl). Pour into a heatproof jug.

4 Dip the end of one stick into the chocolate, then push it about halfway into a ball of cake. Return to tray. Repeat with remaining sticks and balls of cake. Freeze for about 5 minutes to set.

5 Dip one cake pop into the chocolate, rocking back and forth to coat; don't swirl the pop, or it'll break. Allow excess chocolate to drip back into the jug. Slide a straw over the stick, pushing it up into the chocolate. Stand cake pop upright in a styrofoam block (see page 4) until set. Repeat with remaining cake pops. Re-melt chocolate as necessary.

6 Divide royal icing into three small bowls; tint pale blue, pale pink and yellow. Cover surface of icings with plastic wrap to keep them airtight.

7 Spoon blue icing into a small piping bag fitted with a 3mm (⅛-inch) tube. Pipe spirals on top of 10 of the cake pops, turning sticks in the styrofoam as you pipe. Repeat with pink and yellow icing (in clean piping bags) and remaining cake pops. Stand upright until set.

tip Buy drinking
straws in three
colours if you can,
and match them to
their corresponding
cake pops.

Christmas ice-cream pops

- **2 cups (220g) softened vanilla ice-cream**
- **1 cup (200g) christmas pudding, chopped finely**
- **400g (12½-ounce) block dark eating (semi-sweet) chocolate**
- **28 wooden cocktail picks**

tips Make the ice-cream pops 1 or 2 days ahead. Use rounded ice-cube trays if possible. Store ice-cream pops in an airtight container in the freezer until ready to serve. They will keep for up to a week.

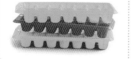

1 Use fingers to lightly oil two 14-hole ice-cube trays. Line a small oven tray with baking paper.

2 Working quickly, combine ice-cream and pudding in a medium bowl; press mixture into ice-cube tray holes. Freeze about 2 hours or until firm. Release cubes onto the prepared tray; freeze 30 minutes.

3 Meanwhile, to make chocolate curls, slightly warm the chocolate block between your hands; drag the blade of a sharp vegetable peeler evenly down the side to give about ¼ cup chocolate curls. Transfer to an airtight container.

4 Chop remaining chocolate. Stir half the chocolate in a medium heatproof bowl over a medium saucepan of simmering water until smooth (don't let water touch base of bowl). Pour into a heatproof jug.

5 Working quickly, insert cocktail picks into ice-cream cubes. Dip half the ice-cream pops, one at a time, into chocolate until covered; return to baking paper-lined tray. Freeze until ready to serve.

6 Repeat melting and dipping with remaining chocolate and ice-cream pops; freeze until ready to serve. Serve pops in paper cases, sprinkled with chocolate curls.

circus clowns

- 1¼ cups (220g) firmly packed madeira cake crumbs
- 2 teaspoons strawberry jam
- 300g (9½ ounces) white chocolate Melts
- 10 lollipop or paddle pop sticks
- 10 mini ice-cream cones
- 2 tablespoons hundreds and thousands
- 10 jaffas
- 30cm (12-inch) length strawberry licorice bootlaces
- 20 pink mini M&M'S
- ¼ quantity royal icing (see page 74)
- black food colouring
- 28g (1 ounce) pink Nerds

makes 10
prep + cook time 1 hour (+ freezing & standing)
store cake pops in an airtight container at a cool room temperature until ready to serve. They will keep for up to a week. Pipe eyes on the day of serving. Don't refrigerate, or the colouring in the decorations will run.

1 Using a fork, combine cake crumbs and jam in a small bowl. Shape level tablespoons of mixture into balls, squeezing firmly. Place balls on a baking paper-lined tray; freeze 1 hour or refrigerate 3 hours or overnight, until firm.
2 Stir chocolate in a medium heatproof bowl over a medium saucepan of simmering water until smooth (don't let water touch base of bowl). Pour into a heatproof jug.
3 Dip the end of one stick into chocolate, then push it about halfway into a ball of cake. Return to tray. Repeat with remaining sticks and balls of cake. Place in the freezer for about 5 minutes to set.
4 Dip a cake pop into the chocolate, rocking back and forth to coat; don't swirl the pop, or it'll break. Allow excess chocolate to drip back into the jug. Stand cake pop upright in a styrofoam block (see page 4) until set. Repeat with remaining cake pops. Re-melt chocolate as necessary.

5 Carefully trim 4.5cm (1¾ inches) from the wide end of the cones, discard trimmings. Dip the cut edge and tip of one (now smaller) cone in chocolate then dip in hundreds and thousands. Place cone on top of a cake pop to make the clown's hat. Hold cone in place for about a minute or until just set. Repeat with remaining cones, chocolate and hundreds and thousands. Stand upright until set.
6 Using a little melted chocolate, secure jaffa noses onto the clowns. Cut licorice into 12 x 2cm (¾-inch) lengths; secure a piece onto each clown to form the mouth. Secure two mini M&M's on each clown for the rosy cheeks.
7 Tint royal icing black. Spoon icing into a piping bag fitted with a 3mm (⅛-inch) tube. Pipe crosses for the eyes. To make hair, secure Nerds near the cone using a little more of the chocolate.

tip Use white Candy Melts in place of chocolate Melts for an extra-white finish.

Australia Day lamington pops

- 4½ cups (540g) firmly packed sponge cake crumbs
- ½ cup (150g) ready-made vanilla frosting
- 375g (12 ounces) dark chocolate Melts
- 32 lollipop or paddle pop sticks
- 1½ cups (120g) desiccated coconut

makes 32
prep + cook time 1 hour (+ freezing & standing)
store cake pops in an airtight container at a cool room temperature until ready to serve. They will keep for up to a week.

1 Using a fork, combine cake crumbs and frosting in a medium bowl. Using wet hands, shape level tablespoons of the mixture into balls, squeezing firmly. Place balls on a baking paper-lined tray. Freeze 1 hour, or refrigerate 3 hours or overnight.

2 Melt chocolate in a medium heatproof bowl over a medium saucepan of simmering water until smooth (don't let water touch base of bowl). Transfer to a heatproof jug.

3 Dip the end of one stick into the chocolate, then push it about halfway into a ball of cake. Return to tray. Repeat with remaining sticks and balls of cake. Freeze for about 5 minutes to set.

4 Place coconut in a shallow dish.

5 Dip one cake pop into the chocolate, rocking back and forth to coat; don't swirl the pop, or it'll break. Allow excess chocolate to drip back into the jug. Stand cake pop upright in a styrofoam block (see page 4). Before chocolate sets, sprinkle and press on coconut to cover the pop. Repeat with remaining cake pops. Re-melt chocolate as necessary. Stand upright until set.

bouquets

- 40g (1½ ounces) cream cheese, softened
- 15g (½ ounce) butter, softened
- ⅔ cup (110g) icing (confectioners') sugar
- ½ teaspoon rosewater
- 2½ cups (450g) firmly packed madeira cake crumbs
- 100g (3 ounces) rose turkish delight, chopped finely
- ¼ cup (35g) unsalted, roasted, finely chopped pistachios
- 375g (12 ounces) white chocolate Melts
- 20 lollipop or paddle pop sticks
- 220g (7 ounces) white sugar flowers

makes 20
prep + cook time
1 hour 30 minutes
(+ freezing & standing)

1 Beat cream cheese and butter in a small bowl with an electric mixer until light and fluffy; gradually beat in sifted icing sugar until combined. Beat in rosewater.

2 Stir in cake crumbs, turkish delight and nuts. Using wet hands, shape level tablespoons of the mixture into balls, squeezing firmly. Place balls on a baking paper-lined tray; freeze 1 hour or refrigerate 3 hours or overnight, until firm.

3 Stir chocolate in a medium heatproof bowl over a medium saucepan of simmering water until smooth (don't let water touch base of bowl). Pour into a heatproof jug.

4 Dip the end of one stick into the chocolate, then push it about halfway into a ball of cake. Return to tray. Repeat with remaining sticks and balls of cake. Freeze for about 5 minutes to set.

5 Dip one cake pop into the chocolate, rocking back and forth to coat; don't swirl the pop, or it'll break. Allow excess chocolate to drip back into the jug. Stand pop upright in a styrofoam block (see page 4). Attach flowers to pop. If chocolate sets before all are attached, re-melt chocolate and use a little to attach remaining flowers. Stand upright until set. Repeat with remaining cake pops and flowers.

tips Use lightly oiled scissors to cut turkish delight. You will need about 35 sugar flowers per cake pop. Store cake pops in an airtight container at a cool room temperature until ready to serve. They will keep for a day.

tips Use yellow Candy Melts in place of tinted chocolate Melts, if you like. Store cake pops in an airtight container at a cool room temperature until ready to serve. Pipe stripes, eyes and mouths on the day of serving. They'll keep for up to a week.

honey bees

- 4 cups (680g) firmly packed butter cake crumbs
- ⅓ cup (100g) ready-made vanilla frosting
- 375g (12 ounces) white chocolate Melts
- yellow food colouring
- 18 lollipop or paddle pop sticks
- 1 quantity royal icing (see page 74)
- black food colouring
- 36 pieces (10g) white Milo Duo cereal

makes 18
prep + cook time
1 hour 15 minutes
(+ freezing & standing)

1 Using a fork, combine cake crumbs and frosting in a medium bowl. Shape level tablespoons of the mixture into teardrop shapes, squeezing firmly. Place on a baking paper-lined tray; freeze 1 hour or refrigerate 3 hours or overnight, until firm.

2 Stir chocolate in a medium heatproof bowl over a medium saucepan of simmering water until smooth (don't let water touch base of bowl). Tint chocolate pale yellow. Pour into a heatproof jug.

3 Dip the end of one stick into the chocolate, then push it about halfway into a piece of cake. Return to tray. Repeat with remaining sticks and cake. Place tray in the freezer for about 5 minutes to set.

4 Dip one cake pop into the chocolate, rocking back and forth to coat; don't swirl the pop, or it'll break. Allow excess chocolate to drip back into the jug. Stand cake pop upright in a styrofoam block (see page 4) until set. Repeat with remaining cake pops. Re-melt chocolate as necessary.

5 Tint royal icing black. Spoon icing into a small piping bag fitted with a 3mm (⅛-inch) tube. Pipe stripes, eyes and mouths onto bees. For the wings, secure two cereal pieces onto each bee with a little icing. Stand pops upright until set.

mint chocolate cake pops

- ⅓ cup (80ml) thickened (heavy) cream
- 80g (2½ ounces) dark eating (semi-sweet) chocolate, chopped
- ½ teaspoon peppermint essence
- 2½ cups (400g) firmly packed chocolate mud cake crumbs
- 180g (5½ ounces) dark chocolate Melts
- 375g (12 ounces) white Candy Melts
- green food colouring
- 27 lollipop or paddle pop sticks

makes 27
prep + cook time
1 hour 15 minutes
(+ freezing & standing)
store cake pops in an airtight container in the fridge until ready to serve. They will keep for up to a week.

1 Bring cream to the boil in a small saucepan; remove from heat. Add chopped chocolate and essence, stand 2 minutes; stir until smooth.

2 Stir chocolate mixture into cake crumbs in a medium bowl. Using wet hands, shape level tablespoons of the mixture into balls, squeezing firmly. Place balls on a baking paper-lined tray. Freeze 1 hour, or refrigerate 3 hours or overnight, until set.

3 Stir dark chocolate Melts in a medium heatproof bowl over a medium saucepan of simmering water until smooth (don't let base of bowl touch water). Transfer to a heatproof jug. Stir Candy Melts in medium heatproof bowl as above; divide Melts between two heatproof jugs. Tint one pale green with food colouring.

4 Dip the end of one stick into the chocolate, then push the stick about halfway into a ball of cake. Return to tray. Repeat with another 8 sticks and balls of cake. Do the same with remaining sticks, balls of cake and green and white Candy Melts. Place tray in freezer for about 5 minutes to set.

5 Re-melt dark chocolate if necessary. Dip 9 cake pops, one at a time, in the chocolate; rocking back and forth to coat; don't swirl the pops, or they'll break. Allow excess chocolate to drip back into the jug. Stand pops upright in a styrofoam block (see page 4) until set. Repeat with green and white Candy Melts.

6 Spoon remaining chocolate and Melts into 3 piping bags fitted with 3mm (⅛-inch) tubes. Drizzle chocolate and Melts over balls as pictured. Stand at room temperature until set.

tip Use white Candy Melts in place of chocolate Melts for an extra-white finish.

daisies

- 40g (1½ ounces) cream cheese, softened
- 15g (½ ounce) butter, softened
- ½ teaspoon vanilla extract
- ⅔ cup (110g) icing (confectioners') sugar
- 2½ cups (450g) firmly packed madeira cake crumbs
- 375g (12 ounces) white chocolate Melts
- 20 lollipop or paddle pop sticks
- 120 (50g) white mini mallows
- 20 mini yellow M&M's
- 10 mint leaf lollies, halved

makes 20
prep + cook time 1 hour (+ freezing & standing)
store cake pops in an airtight container at a cool room temperature until ready to serve. They will keep for up to 2 days.

1 Beat cream cheese, butter and extract in a small bowl with an electric mixer until light and fluffy; gradually beat in sifted icing sugar.

2 Using a fork, combine cream cheese mixture and crumbs in a medium bowl. Using wet hands, roll level tablespoons of mixture into balls, squeezing firmly. Place balls on a baking paper-lined tray. Freeze 1 hour, or refrigerate 3 hours or overnight, until firm.

3 Melt chocolate in a medium heatproof bowl over a medium saucepan of simmering water (don't let water touch base of bowl). Transfer to a heatproof jug.

4 Dip the end of one stick into chocolate, then push it about halfway into a ball of cake. Return to tray. Repeat with remaining sticks and balls of cake. Place tray in the freezer for about 5 minutes to set.

5 Using a rolling pin, flatten mallows.

6 Decorate about four cake pops at a time. Dip the pops into the chocolate, rocking back and forth to coat; don't swirl the pops, or they'll break. Allow excess chocolate to drip back into the jug. Re-melt chocolate as necessary. Stand cake pops upright in a styrofoam block (see page 4). Before chocolate on pops completely sets, decorate with mallows and M&M's. Stand cake pops upright until set.

7 Slide mint leaves onto sticks.

Halloween black spiders

- 2½ cups (400g) firmly packed chocolate mud cake crumbs
- ½ cup (150g) ready-made milk chocolate frosting
- 375g (12 ounces) dark chocolate Melts
- 22 lollipop or paddle pop sticks
- 4.5 metres (4½ yards) licorice bootlaces
- 44 mini M&M's

1 Using a fork, combine cake crumbs and frosting in a medium bowl. Using wet hands, shape mixture into 22 balls, squeezing firmly. Place balls on a baking paper-lined tray.

2 Stir chocolate in a medium heatproof bowl over a medium saucepan of simmering water until smooth (don't let water touch base of bowl). Pour into a heatproof jug.

3 Dip the end of one stick into the chocolate, then push it about halfway into a ball of cake. Return to tray. Repeat with remaining sticks and balls of cake. Place in the freezer for about 5 minutes to set.

4 Cut licorice into 2.5cm (1-inch) lengths.

5 Re-melt chocolate as necessary. Decorate about four cake pops at a time. Dip the cake pops in the chocolate, rocking back and forth to coat; don't swirl the pops, or they'll break. Allow excess chocolate to drip back into the jug. Stand pops upright in a styrofoam block (see page 4) about 30 seconds or until firm enough to hold licorice in place. Insert eight licorice pieces into sides of each pop for legs. Decorate with M&M's for eyes. Stand upright until set.

tip Store cake pops in an airtight container at a cool room temperature until ready to serve. They will keep for up to a week. Don't refrigerate, as the colouring in the M&M's will run.

makes 22
prep + cook time 1 hour
(+ freezing & standing)

tip We used a purchased 800g (1½-pound) fruit cake. Light or dark fruit cake is suitable; use whichever you prefer.

Christmas puddings

- 180g (5½ ounces) dark eating (semi-sweet) chocolate, chopped coarsely
- 800g (1½ pounds) fruit cake
- ½ cup (125ml) brandy
- ½ cup (80g) icing (confectioners') sugar
- 36 lollipop or paddle pop sticks
- 1 quantity royal icing (see page 74)
- 36 red candy-coated chocolates (sixlets)

makes 36
prep + cook time 1 hour (+ freezing & standing)
store pudding pops in an airtight container at a cool room temperature until ready to serve. They will keep for up to a week.

1 Stir chocolate in a medium heatproof bowl over a medium saucepan of simmering water until smooth (don't let water touch base of bowl).
2 Using hands, crumble cake into a large bowl; stir in chocolate, brandy and sifted icing sugar. Using wet hands, shape level tablespoons of mixture into balls, squeezing firmly. Place balls on a baking paper-lined tray. Freeze 1 hour or refrigerate 3 hours or overnight, until firm.

3 Dip the end of one stick into the royal icing, then push it about halfway into a ball of cake. Return to tray. Repeat with remaining sticks and balls of cake. Freeze for about 5 minutes to set.
4 Drizzle royal icing over cake balls, top each with a chocolate; stand pops upright in a styrofoam block (see page 4) until set.

Christmas winter trees

- 8 mini waffle cones
- 3⅓ cups (600g) madeira cake crumbs
- ⅓ cup (115g) strawberry jam
- 375g (12 ounces) white chocolate Melts
- green food colouring
- 8 lollipop or paddle pop sticks
- 1 tablespoon silver cachous
- 8 white icing star toppers

makes 8
prep + cook time
40 minutes
(+ freezing & standing)

1 Carefully cut 2.5cm (1 inch) off the wide end of each cone; discard the trimmings.

2 Using a fork, combine cake crumbs and jam in a medium bowl. Spoon mixture into cones; press down firmly. Place cones on a baking paper-lined tray. Freeze 1 hour or refrigerate 3 hours or overnight, until set.

3 Stir chocolate in a medium heatproof bowl over a medium saucepan of simmering water until smooth (don't let water touch base of bowl). Tint chocolate green. Pour into a heatproof jug.

4 Dip the end of one stick into the chocolate, then push it about halfway into the base of a cone of cake. Return to tray. Repeat with remaining sticks and cones of cake. Place tray in the freezer for about 5 minutes to set.

5 Spoon chocolate all over a cone to coat; allow excess chocolate to drip back into the jug. Stand upright in a styrofoam block (see page 4) until almost set. Attach cachous and an icing star, using a little extra melted chocolate if you need. Repeat with remaining cones, chocolate, cachous and stars. Re-melt chocolate as necessary. Stand upright until set.

tips Store trees in an airtight container at a cool room temperature until ready to serve. They will keep for up to a week. Icing stars can be purchased at cake decorating suppliers.

tips Possums, without eyes, can be made up to two days ahead. Store in an airtight container. Pipe eyes on the day of serving.

possums

- 4 cups (720g) firmly packed chocolate madeira cake crumbs
- ⅓ cup (100g) ready-made rich chocolate fudge frosting
- 375g (12 ounces) white chocolate Melts
- 28 x 15cm (6-inch) bamboo skewers
- 150g (4½ ounces) white chocolate Melts, extra
- brown food colouring
- ¼ cup (50g) white sprinkles
- 168 x 1.5cm (¾-inch) lengths vermicelli noodles
- 4 pink musk or fruit sticks, sliced thinly
- 56 pink mini mallows
- ½ quantity royal icing (see page 74)
- black food colouring
- 28 brown jumbo chenille sticks or pipe cleaners

makes 28
prep + cook time
1 hour 20 minutes
(+ freezing & standing)

1 Using a fork, combine cake crumbs and frosting in a medium bowl. Shape level tablespoons of mixture into balls, squeezing firmly. Place balls on a baking paper-lined tray; freeze 1 hour or refrigerate 3 hours or overnight, until firm.
2 Stir chocolate in a medium heatproof bowl over a medium saucepan of simmering water until smooth (don't let water touch base of bowl). Pour into a heatproof jug.
3 Dip the end of one skewer into the chocolate then push it about halfway into a ball of cake. Return to tray. Repeat with remaining skewers and balls of cake. Place tray in the freezer for about 5 minutes to set.
4 Dip one cake pop into the chocolate, rocking back and forth to coat; don't swirl the pop, or it'll break. Allow excess chocolate to drip back into the jug. Stand cake pop upright in a styrofoam block (see page 4) until set. Repeat with remaining cake pops. Re-melt chocolate as necessary.

5 Stir extra chocolate in a medium heatproof bowl over a medium saucepan of simmering water until smooth (don't let water touch base of bowl). Tint chocolate pale brown. Half-dip the pops into brown chocolate; scatter with sprinkles. Stand pops upright until set.
6 To make whiskers, attach six vermicelli pieces to the white side of each pop with a little of the remaining white chocolate. Top each with a musk stick slice for a nose. To make ears, flatten mallows with a rolling pin then secure two on each pop with white chocolate. Tint royal icing black; spoon into a small piping bag fitted with a 3mm (⅛-inch) tube. Pipe eyes onto pops. Stand upright until set.
7 Twist chenille sticks around skewers.

swirly lollipops

- 4 cups (680g) firmly packed orange cake crumbs
- ⅓ cup (100g) ready-made vanilla frosting
- 425g (13½ ounces) white chocolate Melts
- pink food colouring
- 38 lollipop sticks or bamboo skewers
- 38 coloured drinking straws

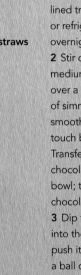

1 Using a fork, combine cake crumbs and frosting in a medium bowl. Shape 3 level teaspoons of mixture into balls, squeezing firmly. Place balls on a baking paper-lined tray; freeze 1 hour, or refrigerate 3 hours or overnight, until firm.
2 Stir chocolate in a medium heatproof bowl over a medium saucepan of simmering water until smooth (don't let water touch base of bowl). Transfer two-thirds of the chocolate into a small bowl; tint remaining chocolate pale pink.
3 Dip the end of one stick into the chocolate, then push it about halfway into a ball of cake. Return to tray. Repeat with remaining sticks and balls of cake. Freeze for about 5 minutes to set.

4 Dip one cake pop into the white chocolate, rocking back and forth to coat; don't swirl the pop, or it'll break. Allow excess chocolate to drip back into the jug. While cake pop is still wet, drizzle a little of the pink chocolate over the top, swirling pop until smooth. Slide a straw over the stick, pushing it up into the chocolate. Stand cake pop upright in a styrofoam block (see page 4) until set. Repeat with remaining cake pops. Re-melt chocolate as necessary.

makes 38
prep + cook time 1 hour
(+ freezing & standing)

tip Store cake pops in an airtight container at a cool room temperature until ready to serve. They will keep for up to a week.

Easter egg pops

- 4 cups (640g) firmly packed chocolate cake crumbs
- ⅓ cup (100g) ready-made milk chocolate frosting
- 375g (12 ounces) white Candy Melts
- purple, yellow, green and blue food colouring
- 18 lollipop or paddle pop sticks
- 1 tablespoon each purple, yellow, green and blue sanding sugar

makes 18
prep + cook time 50 minutes
(+ freezing & standing)
store cake pops in an airtight container at a cool room temperature until ready to serve. Don't refrigerate or the sugar will dissolve. They will keep for up to a week.

1 Using a fork, combine cake crumbs and frosting in a medium bowl. Shape level tablespoons of the mixture into ovals, squeezing firmly. Place ovals on a baking paper-lined tray; freeze 1 hour, or refrigerate 3 hours or overnight, until firm.

2 Stir Candy Melts in a medium heatproof bowl over a medium saucepan of simmering water until smooth (don't let water touch base of bowl). Divide Melts evenly between four small bowls; tint pale purple, yellow, green and blue.

3 Dip the end of one stick into the Melts, then push the stick about halfway into an oval of cake. Return to tray. Repeat with remaining sticks and ovals of cake, alternating colours. Freeze for about 5 minutes to set.

4 Dip one cake pop into the purple Melts, rocking back and forth to coat; don't swirl the pop, or it'll break. Allow excess to drip back into the bowl. Stand cake pop upright in a styrofoam block (see page 4) until set. Repeat with remaining cake pops, alternating the colours. Re-melt Candy Melts as necessary.

5 Working with one colour at a time, spoon remaining Melts into small piping bags. Pipe dots onto cake pops, then press the corresponding coloured sugar onto the dots. We used blue sugar on purple eggs, yellow sugar on blue eggs, green sugar on yellow eggs and purple sugar on green eggs. Stand upright until set.

rainbow moon rocks

- 1¼ cups (220g) firmly packed madeira cake crumbs
- 1½ tablespoons apricot jam
- 300g (9½ ounces) white chocolate Melts
- green food colouring
- 14 lollipop or paddle pop sticks
- 3 cups (35g) coloured sugared popcorn

> makes 14
> prep + cook time 45 minutes (+ freezing & standing)

1 Using a fork, combine cake crumbs and jam in a small bowl. Shape level tablespoons of mixture into balls, squeezing firmly. Place balls on a baking paper-lined tray; freeze 1 hour or refrigerate 3 hours or overnight, until firm.

2 Stir chocolate in a medium heatproof bowl over a medium saucepan of simmering water until smooth (don't let water touch base of bowl). Tint chocolate green. Pour into a heatproof jug.

3 Dip the end of one stick into the chocolate, then push it about halfway into a ball of cake. Return to tray. Repeat with remaining sticks and balls of cake. Freeze for about 5 minutes to set.

4 Break popcorn into small pieces.

5 Dip one cake pop into the chocolate, rocking back and forth to coat; don't swirl the pop, or it'll break. Allow excess chocolate to drip back into the jug. Press on popcorn to cover surface. Stand cake pop upright in a styrofoam block (see page 4) until set. Repeat with remaining pops, chocolate and popcorn; re-melt chocolate as necessary.

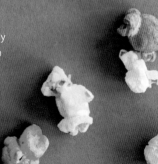

tip Store cake pops in an airtight container at a cool room temperature until ready to serve. They will keep for up to a week.

tips Use white Candy Melts in place of chocolate Melts for a whiter finish. Store cake pops in an airtight container at a cool room temperature until ready to serve. They will keep for up to a week.

New Year's Eve glitter balls

- **4 cups (680g) firmly packed butter cake crumbs**
- **⅓ cup (100g) ready-made vanilla frosting**
- **275g (9 ounces) white chocolate Melts**
- **38 lollipop or paddle pop sticks**
- **5g (¼ ounce) hologram silver edible glitter**

makes 38
prep + cook time 1 hour
(+ freezing & standing)

1 Using a fork, combine cake crumbs and frosting in a medium bowl. Shape three level teaspoons of mixture at a time into balls, squeezing firmly. Place balls on a baking paper-lined tray; freeze 1 hour or refrigerate 3 hours or overnight, until firm.

2 Stir chocolate in a medium heatproof bowl over a medium saucepan of simmering water until smooth (don't let water touch base of bowl). Pour into a heatproof jug.

3 Dip the end of one stick into the chocolate, then push it about halfway into a ball of cake. Return to tray. Repeat with remaining sticks and balls of cake. Freeze for about 5 minutes to set.

4 Dip one cake pop into the chocolate, rocking back and forth to coat; don't swirl the pop, or it'll break. Allow excess chocolate to drip back into the jug. Sprinkle the pop with glitter. Stand upright in a styrofoam block (see page 4) until set. Repeat with remaining cake pops. Re-melt chocolate as necessary.

cappuccino pops

- 300g (9½ ounces) cream-filled chocolate biscuits, chopped coarsely
- 1 cup (300g) ready-made rich chocolate fudge frosting
- 375g (12 ounces) white chocolate Melts
- 25 bamboo skewers
- 25 large coffee-flavoured chocolate buttons
- 68g (2 ounces) peppermint Life Savers
- ½ cup (50g) hot chocolate flakes

makes 25
prep + cook time 1 hour
(+ freezing & standing)

1 Process biscuits until fine. Using a fork, combine crumbs and frosting in a medium bowl. Shape level tablespoons of the mixture into balls, squeezing firmly. Place on a baking paper-lined tray; freeze 1 hour or refrigerate 3 hours or overnight, until firm.
2 Stir white chocolate in a medium heatproof bowl over a medium saucepan of simmering water until smooth (don't let water touch base of bowl). Pour into a heatproof jug.
3 Dip the end of one skewer into the chocolate, then push it about halfway into a ball of cake. Return to tray. Repeat with remaining skewers and balls of cake. Freeze for about 5 minutes to set.

4 To make saucers, place chocolate buttons flat on a board. Using the pointed end of a skewer, gently push a hole, using a twisting motion, through the centre of each button.
5 Using a sharp knife, cut the top-third off balls to create a flat top; discard off-cuts. Dip one cake pop into the chocolate, rocking back and forth to coat; don't swirl the pop, or it'll break. Allow excess chocolate to drip back into the jug. Stand pop upright in a styrofoam block (see page 4). When chocolate is almost set, thread a button onto each stick, pushing up to the base of the cake pop. Repeat with remaining pops. Re-melt chocolate as necessary.
6 Cut Life Savers in half; push into the side of each cake pop to form handles. Sprinkle chocolate flakes over tops of cake pops.

tips Hot chocolate flakes are usually sold in the coffee section of the supermarket. Store cake pops in an airtight container at a cool room temperature until ready to serve. They will keep for up to a week. Top with flakes just before serving.

smiley faces

- **4 cups (720g) firmly packed madeira cake crumbs**
- **2 tablespoons finely grated lemon rind**
- **1 tablespoon lemon juice**
- **¼ cup (75g) ready-made vanilla frosting**
- **275g (9 ounces) white chocolate Melts**
- **yellow food colouring**
- **18 lollipop or paddle pop sticks**
- **¼ quantity royal icing (see page 74)**
- **black food colouring**

makes 18
prep + cook time 1 hour
(+ freezing & standing)
store cake pops in an airtight
container at a cool room
temperature until ready to
serve. Pipe eyes and mouths
on the day of serving. They
will keep for up to a week.

1 Using a fork, combine cake crumbs, rind, juice and frosting in a medium bowl. Press level tablespoons of the mixture into a 5cm (2-inch) round cutter; round the edges with your fingers. Place rounds on a baking paper-lined tray; freeze 1 hour or refrigerate 3 hours or overnight, until firm.

2 Stir chocolate in a medium heatproof bowl over a medium saucepan of simmering water until smooth (don't let water touch base of bowl). Tint chocolate yellow; pour into a heatproof jug.

3 Dip the end of one stick into the chocolate, then push it about halfway into a round of cake. Return to tray. Repeat with remaining sticks and rounds of cake. Freeze for about 5 minutes to set.

4 Dip one cake pop into the chocolate, rocking back and forth to coat; don't swirl the pop, or it'll break. Allow excess chocolate to drip back into the jug. Stand cake pop upright in a styrofoam block (see page 4) until set. Repeat with remaining cake pops. Re-melt chocolate as necessary.

5 Tint royal icing black. Spoon icing into a small piping bag fitted with a 3mm (⅛-inch) tube; pipe eyes and mouths onto rounds. Stand pops upright until set.

coconut pops

- 40g (1½ ounces) cream cheese, softened
- 15g (½ ounce) butter, softened
- ⅔ cup (110g) icing (confectioners') sugar
- 2 tablespoons coconut rum or coconut liqueur
- 2 teaspoons finely grated lime rind
- 4½ cups (450g) firmly packed sponge cake crumbs
- 375g (12 ounces) white chocolate Melts
- 20 lollipop or paddle pop sticks
- 1 cup (100g) moist coconut flakes

makes 20
prep + cook time 1 hour
(+ freezing & standing)

1 Beat cream cheese and butter in a small bowl with electric mixer until light and fluffy; gradually beat in sifted icing sugar.
2 Using a fork, combine cream cheese mixture, rum and rind into cake crumbs in a medium bowl. Using wet hands, shape rounded tablespoons of mixture into balls, squeezing firmly. Place balls on a baking paper-lined tray; freeze 1 hour or refrigerate 3 hours or overnight, until firm.
3 Stir chocolate in a medium heatproof bowl over a medium saucepan of simmering water until smooth (don't let base of bowl touch water). Pour into a heatproof jug.

4 Dip the end of one stick into the chocolate, then push it about halfway into a ball of cake. Return to tray. Repeat with remaining sticks and balls of cake. Freeze for about 5 minutes to set.
5 Dip one cake pop into the chocolate, rocking back and forth to coat; don't swirl the pop, or it'll break. Allow excess chocolate to drip back into the jug. Stand pop upright in a styrofoam block (see page 4). When chocolate has almost set, press coconut flakes onto cake pop to cover. Stand upright to set. Repeat with remaining cake pops and coconut. Re-melt chocolate as necessary.

tips Use white Candy Melts in place of chocolate Melts for an extra-white finish. Store cake pops in the refrigerator until ready to serve. They will keep for up to a week.

tips Use white chocolate Melts and pink food colouring in place of the pink Candy Melts, if you like. Store cake pops in an airtight container at a cool room temperature until ready to serve. They will keep for up to a week.

glazed caramel doughnuts

- **3½ cups (560g) firmly packed caramel mud cake crumbs**
- **1 tablespoon ready-made rich chocolate fudge frosting**
- **100g (3 ounces) dark (semi-sweet) chocolate Melts**
- **100g (3 ounces) pink Candy Melts**
- **¼ cup (60g) hundreds and thousands**
- **16 lollipop or paddle pop sticks**

makes 16
prep + cook time
45 minutes
(+ freezing & standing)

1 Using a fork, combine cake crumbs and frosting in a medium bowl. Using wet hands, shape level tablespoons of mixture into balls, squeezing firmly. Press mixture into a 4.5cm (1¾-inch) cutter to form a round. Using the end of a wooden spoon, press a hole in the centre of each round. Carefully transfer rings to a baking paper-lined tray; freeze 1 hour or refrigerate 3 hours or overnight, until firm.

2 Stir dark chocolate in a medium heatproof bowl over a medium saucepan of simmering water until smooth (don't let water touch base of bowl). Repeat for Candy Melts.

3 Spoon a small amount of the melted chocolate or Candy Melts over rings; scatter with hundreds and thousands. Return to trays. Stand at room temperature until completely set. Insert sticks.

tips Any small jubes or jelly sweets can be used. Use lightly oiled scissors to cut the jubes. Store cake pops in an airtight container at a cool room temperature until ready to serve. They will keep for up to a week.

stained glass cake pops

- 1⅓ cups (230g) firmly packed butter cake crumbs
- 1½ tablespoons apricot jam
- 300g (9½ ounces) white chocolate Melts
- 18 lollipop or paddle pop sticks
- 200g (5½ ounces) jubes, sliced thinly

makes 18
prep + cook time 1½ hours
(+ freezing & standing)

1 Using a fork, combine cake crumbs and jam in a medium bowl. Shape 2 level teaspoons of mixture into balls, squeezing firmly. Place on a baking paper- lined tray; freeze 1 hour or refrigerate 3 hours or overnight, until firm.
2 Stir chocolate in a medium heatproof bowl over a medium saucepan of simmering water until smooth (don't let water touch base of bowl). Transfer to a heatproof jug.
3 Dip the end of one stick into the chocolate, then push it about halfway into a ball of cake. Return to tray. Repeat with remaining sticks and balls of cake. Freeze for about 5 minutes to set.

4 Decorate about four cake pops at a time. Dip the pops into the chocolate, rocking back and forth to coat; don't swirl the pops, or they'll break. Allow excess chocolate to drip back into the jug. Re-melt chocolate as necessary. Stand cake pops upright in a styrofoam block (see page 4). Before chocolate on pops completely sets, cover with jube slices. Stand cake pops upright until set.

chocolate tiramisu cups

- 200g (6½ ounces) dark (semi-sweet) chocolate Melts
- 20 foil petit four cases
- 20 bamboo skewers
- ⅓ cup (125g) mascarpone cheese
- ⅓ cup (80ml) coffee liqueur
- 100g (3 ounces) sponge cake
- 20 dark (semi-sweet) chocolate-coated coffee beans
- 2 tablespoons cocoa powder

makes 20
prep + cook time
1 hour (+ refrigeration)

1 Stir chocolate in small heatproof bowl over a small saucepan of simmering water until smooth (don't let water touch base of bowl). Using a paintbrush, paint melted chocolate thickly on inside of the foil cases. Place on a tray. Refrigerate 30 minutes or until set. Reserve leftover chocolate.

2 Gently peel away foil cases from chocolate. Place chocolate cups flat on bench. Using the pointed end of a skewer, gently push a hole, using a twisting motion, through the centre of the base of each chocolate cup. Re-melt chocolate; paint a second coat, avoiding the holes. Return to tray, refrigerate until set. Reserve remaining chocolate.

3 Re-melt reserved chocolate. Remove chocolate cups from the refrigerator; turn upside-down on a baking paper-lined tray.

Dip the end of one skewer in the chocolate, then gently push it through the hole of a cup, ensuring the skewer remains straight. Repeat with remaining skewers and cups. Transfer to refrigerator; allow to set completely.

4 Stir mascarpone and 1 tablespoon of the liqueur in a small bowl until combined. Pour remaining liqueur into a small shallow bowl. Cut cake into 1cm (½-inch) cubes. Dip cubes of cake into liqueur, one at a time, then thread onto the skewer inside each chocolate cup. Stand pops upright in a styrofoam block (see page 4). Top each cup with a small dollop of the mascarpone mixture and a coffee bean. Just before serving, dust with sifted cocoa.

tip Store tiramisu cups upright in the refrigerator until ready to serve. They are best made on the day of serving.

makes 24
prep + cook time
1 hour 20 minutes
(+ freezing & standing)
store cake pops in an
airtight container at a cool
room temperature until
ready to serve. They will
keep for up to a week.

building blocks

- **4 cups (680g) firmly packed butter cake crumbs**
- **⅓ cup (100g) ready-made vanilla frosting**
- **375g (12 ounces) white chocolate Melts**
- **24 lollipop or paddle pop sticks**
- **1 quantity royal icing (see page 74)**
- **pink, yellow and blue food colouring**

tips You'll have one leftover cube of cake – practise your piping on this if you like. Use white Candy Melts in place of chocolate Melts for an extra-white finish.

1 Line base and sides of a 20cm (8-inch) square cake pan with baking paper. Using a fork, combine cake crumbs and frosting in a medium bowl. Press mixture into the pan. Freeze 1 hour or refrigerate 3 hours or overnight, until firm. Lift mixture from pan; cut into 4cm x 4cm (1½-inch x 1½-inch) cubes.
2 Stir chocolate in a medium heatproof bowl over a medium saucepan of simmering water until smooth (don't let water touch base of bowl). Pour into a heatproof jug.
3 Dip the end of one stick into the chocolate, then push it about halfway into a cube of cake. Place on a baking paper-lined tray. Repeat with remaining sticks and cubes of cake. Place tray in the freezer for about 5 minutes to set.

4 Dip the cake pops into the chocolate, rocking back and forth to coat; don't swirl the pops, or they will break. Allow excess to drip back into the jug. Stand cake pops upright in a styrofoam block (see page 4) until set. Re-melt chocolate as necessary.
5 Divide royal icing between three small bowls; tint pale pink, yellow and blue. Cover surface of icings with plastic wrap to keep them airtight. Spoon pink icing into a small piping bag fitted with a 3mm (⅛-inch) tube. Pipe borders on each side of eight cubes to define edges; pipe letters inside the borders. Repeat with yellow and blue icing (in clean piping bags) and remaining cubes. Stand upright until set.

crazy straw pops

- 4 cups (680g) firmly packed butter cake crumbs
- ⅓ cup (100g) ready-made rich chocolate fudge frosting
- 375g (12 ounces) white chocolate Melts
- 28 decorative drinking straws
- 1¼ cups (275g) coloured sprinkles (we used ¼ cup each of dark blue, light blue, orange, pink and yellow)

makes 28
prep + cook time
40 minutes
(+ freezing & standing)
store cake pops in an airtight container at a cool room temperature until ready to serve. They will keep for up to a week.

1 Using a fork, combine cake crumbs and frosting in a medium bowl. Shape level tablespoons of mixture into balls, squeezing firmly. Place balls on a baking paper-lined tray; freeze 1 hour or refrigerate 3 hours or overnight, until firm.

2 Stir chocolate in a medium heatproof bowl over a medium saucepan of simmering water until smooth (don't let water touch base of bowl). Pour into a heatproof jug.

3 Dip the curly end of one straw into the chocolate, then push the straw about halfway into a ball of cake. Return to tray. Repeat with remaining straws and balls of cake. Freeze for about 5 minutes to set.

4 Decorate about four cake pops at a time. Dip the pops into the chocolate, rocking back and forth to coat; don't swirl the pops, or they'll break. Allow excess chocolate to drip back into the jug. Stand cake pops upright in a styrofoam block (see page 4) until almost set. Place sprinkles in small bowls. Before chocolate completely sets, dip cake pops in sprinkles, turning pops to cover surface. Stand upright until set. Repeat with remaining cake pops. Re-melt chocolate as necessary.

royal icing

- 1½ cups (240g) pure icing (confectioners') sugar, approximately
- 1 egg white
- ¼ teaspoon strained lemon juice

1 Sift icing sugar through a fine sieve.
2 Lightly beat egg white in a small bowl with an electric mixer until mixture is just broken up – don't whip into peaks.
3 Beat in the icing sugar, one tablespoon at a time, until the icing reaches a soft, spoonable consistency.
4 Mix in the juice using a wooden spoon.
Cover surface of icing with plastic wrap to keep airtight.

tips If you want to make small amounts of royal icing, use a teaspoon of lightly beaten egg white, then stir in enough icing sugar to make the required consistency. You can buy a royal icing mix from some supermarkets and cake decorating suppliers. Royal icing will keep at a cool room temperature for several days.

buttercream

- **125g (4 ounces) butter, softened**
- **1½ cups (240g) icing (confectioners') sugar**
- **2 tablespoons milk**

1 Beat butter (and any flavouring, if using) in a small narrow bowl with an electric mixer until as white as possible.

2 Gradually beat in half the sifted icing sugar, then milk, then the remaining sifted icing sugar.

3 Beat until the buttercream is smooth and spreadable. Keep scraping down the side of the bowl while beating.

tip Beating the butter until it whitens will give you better results when colouring the buttercream.

glossary

ALMONDS, FLAKED
paper-thin slices.

BAKING PAPER also called
parchment, silicon paper or
non-stick baking paper; not to
be confused with greaseproof
paper. Used to line cake pans
and make piping bags.

BUTTER we use salted butter
unless stated otherwise.

unsalted or "sweet" butter
has no added salt.

CACHOUS also known as
dragées; minuscule (3mm to
5mm) metallic looking yet
edible confectionery balls are
available in silver, gold and
some colours.

CANDY MELTS available from
cake decorating suppliers; are
easy-to-melt discs that are
ideal for dipping and coating.
They come in a variety of
colours and flavours and melt
in the same way as chocolate.

CHOCOLATE
Choc Bits also called
chocolate chips or chocolate
morsels; available in milk,
white and dark chocolate.

dark eating also called
semi-sweet or luxury
chocolate; made of a high
percentage of cocoa liquor
and cocoa butter, with little
added sugar.

Melts small discs of compound
milk, white or dark chocolate
ideal for melting and moulding.

white eating contains no
cocoa solids but derives its
sweet flavour from cocoa
butter. Very sensitive to heat.

COCONUT
desiccated dried, unsweetened,
finely shredded coconut flesh.

moist flakes sweetened,
moistened coconut flakes.

shredded unsweetened thin
strips of dried coconut flesh.

CORNFLOUR also known as
cornstarch. Available made
from corn or wheat (wheaten
cornflour, gluten-free, gives a
lighter texture in cakes); used
as a thickening agent.

CREAM
pouring also called pure
cream; has no additives.

thickened a whipping cream
that contains a thickener.

EGGS we use large chicken
eggs (60g) in our recipes
unless stated otherwise. If a
recipe calls for raw or barely
cooked eggs, exercise
caution if there is a salmonella
problem in your area.

FLOUR
plain also called all-purpose;
unbleached wheat flour is the
best for baking.

self-raising all-purpose plain or
wholemeal flour with baking
powder and salt added.

strong baker's also known as
gluten-enriched, baker's or
bread-mix flour. Produced
from a variety of wheat that
has a high gluten (protein)
content and is best suited for
pizza and bread making. It is
available from supermarkets
and health food stores.

FOOD COLOURING
vegetable-based substance
available in liquid, paste or
gel form.

JAM also called conserve
or preserve.

LOLLIES also called sweets
or candy.

MILO DUOS malt- and
vanilla-flavoured cereal curls,
available in supermarkets.

READY-MADE FROSTING
also known as creamy deluxe
frosting. Found in the baking
section of most supermarkets;
ready to spread straight from
the tub. Available in flavours
such as rich chocolate fudge,
milk chocolate and vanilla.

READY-MADE WHITE ICING
also knowwn as ready-to-roll
icing (RTR), fondant icing,
sugar paste, plastic icing and
soft icing. Is sweet tasting,
and has a dough-like
consistency when kneaded.
Used to cover cakes and
make decorations. Available
from the baking section in
most supermarkets.

ROSEWATER extract made
from crushed rose petals;
used for its aromatic quality in
many desserts. Don't confuse
with rose essence, which is
more concentrated.

STYROFOAM a tightly-packed
polystyrene foam that resists
moisture. It is available in
different-shaped blocks from
cake decorating and craft
supply stores.

SUGAR we use coarse,
granulated table sugar, unless
stated otherwise.

caster also called superfine or
finely granulated table sugar.

icing also called confectioners'
sugar or powdered sugar;
pulverised granulated sugar
crushed together with a small
amount of cornflour.

VERMICELLI NOODLES dried
rice noodles.

conversion chart

measures

One Australian metric measuring cup holds approximately 250ml, one Australian metric tablespoon holds 20ml, one Australian metric teaspoon holds 5ml. The difference between one country's measuring cups and another's is within a 2- or 3-teaspoon variance, and will not affect your cooking results. North America, New Zealand and the United Kingdom use a 15ml tablespoon. All cup and spoon measurements are level. The most accurate way of measuring dry ingredients is to weigh them. When measuring liquids, use a clear glass or plastic jug with metric markings. We use large eggs with an average weight of 60g.

dry measures

METRIC	IMPERIAL
15g	½oz
30g	1oz
60g	2oz
90g	3oz
125g	4oz (¼lb)
155g	5oz
185g	6oz
220g	7oz
250g	8oz (½lb)
280g	9oz
315g	10oz
345g	11oz
375g	12oz (¾lb)
410g	13oz
440g	14oz
470g	15oz
500g	16oz (1lb)
750g	24oz (1½lb)
1kg	32oz (2lb)

liquid measures

METRIC	IMPERIAL
30ml	1 fluid oz
60ml	2 fluid oz
100ml	3 fluid oz
125ml	4 fluid oz
150ml	5 fluid oz
190ml	6 fluid oz
250ml	8 fluid oz
300ml	10 fluid oz
500ml	16 fluid oz
600ml	20 fluid oz
1000ml (1 litre)	1¾ pints

length measures

METRIC	IMPERIAL
3mm	⅛in
6mm	¼in
1cm	½in
2cm	¾in
2.5cm	1in
5cm	2in
6cm	2½in
8cm	3in
10cm	4in
13cm	5in
15cm	6in
18cm	7in
20cm	8in
23cm	9in
25cm	10in
28cm	11in
30cm	12in (1ft)

oven temperatures

These oven temperatures are only a guide for conventional ovens. For fan-forced ovens, check the manufacturer's manual.

	°C (CELSIUS)	°F (FAHRENHEIT)
Very slow	120	250
Slow	150	275-300
Moderately slow	160	325
Moderate	180	350-375
Moderately hot	200	400
Hot	220	425-450
Very hot	240	475

The imperial measurements used in these recipes are approximate only. Measurements for cake pans are approximate only. Using same-shaped cake pans of a similar size should not affect the outcome of your baking. We measure the inside top of the cake pan to determine sizes.

index

Published in 2013 by Bauer Media Books, Sydney
Bauer Media Books are published by Bauer Media Limited
54 Park St, Sydney
GPO Box 4088, Sydney, NSW 2001.
phone (02) 9282 8618; fax (02) 9126 3702
www.awwcookbooks.com.au

MEDIA GROUP

BAUER MEDIA BOOKS
Publisher – Sally Wright
Editorial & Food Director – Pamela Clark
Creative Director – Hieu Chi Nguyen
Food Concept Director – Sophia Young
Director of Sales, Marketing & Rights – Brian Cearnes

Published and Distributed in the United Kingdom by Octopus Publishing Group
Endeavour House
189 Shaftesbury Avenue
London WC2H 8JY
United Kingdom
phone (+44)(0)207 632 5400; fax (+44)(0)207 632 5405
info@octopus-publishing.co.uk;
www.octopusbooks.co.uk

To order books:
telephone LBS on 01903 828 503
order online at
www.australian-womens-weekly.com
or www.octopusbooks.co.uk

Printed in Thailand
International foreign language rights, Brian Cearnes, Bauer Media Books
bcearnes@bauer-media.com.au

A catalogue record for this book is available from the British Library.
ISBN 978-1-74245-283-8
© Bauer Media Limited 2013
ABN 18 053 273 546
This publication is copyright. No part of it may be reproduced or transmitted
in any form without the written permission of the Publisher.
First published in 2013. Reprinted 2013.